MW01537400

Original title:
The Silent Wolf

Author: Eliora Lumiste
ISBN HARDBACK: 978-9908-1-0094-4
ISBN PAPERBACK: 978-9908-1-0095-1
ISBN EBOOK: 978-9908-1-0096-8

Whispers in the Moonlight

Underneath the silver glow,
Laughter dances through the trees,
Colors twirl in soft delight,
Joyful hearts sway with the breeze.

Candles flicker, shadows play,
Voices mingle on warm air,
Starry skies a perfect stage,
Magic whispers everywhere.

Shadows of the Midnight Howl

Crickets chirp a soothing tune,
Fireflies light the midnight air,
Howls arise from cozy dens,
Nature sings without a care.

Fires crackle, friends draw close,
Stories shared beneath the sky,
Moonlit paths invite us all,
To dance and let our spirits fly.

Secrets of the Quiet Prowler

In the hush of night we hear,
Rustling leaves and subtle sighs,
Curious eyes peek from the dark,
Whiskers twitching, secrets rise.

Footsteps soft on mossy ground,
The thrill of chase, the heart's quick beat,
Under stars, adventure calls,
The night is young, the world's a treat.

Echoes in the Twilight Forest

Silhouettes of trees take shape,
In twilight's embrace, shadows dance,
Whispers echo through the woods,
Calling all for a fragrant chance.

Mingle here where spirits play,
With laughter threading through the night,
Joyful tales and songs abound,
A festive scene, a pure delight.

Whispers of the Wild

In the woods, laughter sings,
Beneath the trees, joy takes flight.
Colors dance in autumn's light,
Nature's whispers, pure delight.

Frolic through the golden leaves,
Every rustle sparks a cheer.
Creatures join, the night believes,
In the magic that we hear.

Nightfall's Keeper

Stars emerge, a twinkling show,
Moonlit paths where shadows play.
Laughter echoes, soft and low,
In the warmth of night's ballet.

Glimmers of a distant dream,
Friendship blooms in twilight's glow.
Shared secrets, like a gentle stream,
Underneath the stars we know.

Serenity in the Stillness

Gentle breezes kiss the trees,
Petals scatter, soft and bright.
In this moment, hearts find peace,
Drifting in the soothing light.

Whispers of calm, a tender tune,
Nature's breath, a soft embrace.
Echoing beneath the moon,
Finding joy in every space.

Uncharted Trails of Dusk

Hidden paths invite our feet,
With each turn, a tale unfolds.
Adventures swirl, a dance so sweet,
In the twilight's hues of gold.

Hand in hand, we wander far,
Exploring dreams with every stride.
Guided by the evening star,
Joyous hearts, we turn the tide.

Calls from the Enchanted Woods

Whispers dance in the vibrant leaves,
Joyful laughter the fairies weave.
Glowing lights in the twilight glade,
Magic sings, in shadows played.

Mushrooms glow like lanterns bright,
Guiding hearts with their gentle light.
A symphony of nature's cheer,
Echoes sweetly, drawing near.

Mysteries of the Moonlit Path

Softly shines the silver glow,
Casting dreams where wishes flow.
Eyes of stars wink from above,
Whispers of peace, and endless love.

Shadows play in the cool night air,
Dancing secrets, beyond compare.
Each step leads to wondrous sights,
Where laughter twirls through the nights.

Beneath the Howling Sky

Underneath the tempest's roar,
Joyful spirits rise and soar.
Lightning flashes, a vibrant dance,
We embrace the wild romance.

Rain showers down like sparkling gems,
Nature's rhythm, the heart condemns.
In the chaos, we find our bliss,
Under howling winds, we dare to kiss.

The Solitary Sentinel

A tall tree stands with branches wide,
Guarding secrets the stars confide.
Whirling breezes carry songs,
Celebrating where the heart belongs.

Through changing seasons, steadfast and true,
It marks the passage for me and you.
In its embrace, we laugh and play,
Under the warmth of golden day.

Essential Harmony of Night

Stars twinkle bright in the deep-set sky,
Laughter erupts as we dance and fly.
Songs echo sweet through the cool evening air,
Joy wraps around us, light as a prayer.

Candles flicker, casting warm, gentle glow,
Hearts intertwine, letting pure magic flow.
Whispers of dreams linger soft in the night,
Together we thrive, in pure festive delight.

Hushed Footfalls Amongst the Pines

Through the tall trees where secrets reside,
Footfalls are soft, as hearts beat with pride.
Rustling leaves join in nature's sweet song,
Together we wander, where all souls belong.

The moonlight dapples on pathways ahead,
Sharing warm stories where laughter is spread.
Moments unfold beneath the starlit dome,
In the hush of the night, we find a true home.

Eclipsed by Nature's Breath

Beneath the vast skies, where wonders arise,
Nature's embrace wraps us snug, like a prize.
Colors of twilight blend soft in the air,
Every heartbeat whispers a love we all share.

As shadows grow long in the fading light,
We gather together, hearts full and bright.
The song of the forest, a melody sweet,
In festive enchantment, our souls truly meet.

Veil of the Untold Journey

With lanterns aloft, we tread paths anew,
The air carries laughter, as dreams dapple through.
Beneath the night sky, where wishes take flight,
We dance on the edge of the stars' silver light.

Every step forward, the sparkles ignite,
Voices of joy blend with the cool breeze at night.
Wrapped in the warmth of moments so dear,
In the veil of our journey, we banish all fear.

The Heartbeat of the Hidden Wood

In the forest where laughter sings,
Joyful whispers of nature's wings.
Colors dance beneath the trees,
As the gentle breeze sets hearts at ease.

Flickering lights like stars above,
Every creature shares its love.
A celebration in every shade,
The heart of the wood in jubilant parade.

Festive blooms in vibrant hues,
Each petal tells a tale of muse.
Among the branches, moments abide,
Where joyfulness and peace reside.

Echoes of song in twilight's gleam,
Nature's magic, a radiant dream.
Under the moon's soft, silver glow,
In the hidden wood, our spirits flow.

Unheard Voices in the Still Night

In the hush of night, laughter weaves,
Gentle echoes play among the leaves.
Stars twinkle in playful delight,
With unheard voices dancing in light.

Whispers of secrets float on the air,
Tales of the brave, the bold, the rare.
Moonlit paths beckon hearts to sway,
As shadows of dreams drift softly away.

A tapestry woven of joy and mirth,
Celebrating life, the beauty of earth.
In stillness, the world finds its voice,
In the silence, we too rejoice.

With lanterns aglow, the night ignites,
Festive spirits soar to dizzying heights.
Though unheard, they sing, we feel their song,
In the still night where we all belong.

The Enigma of the Unseen

In the realm where wonders dwell,
Mysteries rise like a hidden spell.
Through veils of night, the magic gleams,
A tapestry woven of vibrant dreams.

Colors pulse in an ethereal dance,
Inviting us all to take a chance.
Beyond the eyes, where spirits play,
In shadows, we lose ourselves and sway.

Voices echo in a rhythmic tide,
Secrets of joy in the heart reside.
Each moment a spark, setting souls free,
In the enigma, we find the key.

Festivities linger on every breeze,
Whispers of joy rustling the trees.
In the unseen, our hearts take flight,
Embracing the magic that colors the night.

The Resilient Echo

Amidst the echoes of joy's refrain,
Resilience dances in sunshine and rain.
Each heartbeat pulses with vibrant grace,
In the rhythm of life, we find our place.

Voices rise in a harmonious swell,
Stories of struggle that only time tells.
Through trials endured, wisdom is gained,
In the resilient echo, hope is sustained.

Festive laughter fills the air,
In moments cherished, love we share.
Together we stand, hand in hand,
In the symphony of life, we make our stand.

Every challenge faced, a step towards light,
Through shadows we weave, we find our flight.
In the echo of courage, hear the call,
In our unity, together we stand tall.

Beneath the Silver Pines

Beneath the silver pines we dance,
Whispers of joy in the moonlit trance.
Stars twinkle bright above our head,
In this magical place, our worries shed.

Laughter echoes through the night,
As fireflies join, a wondrous sight.
We share our dreams, both bold and grand,
Together we weave like wisps of sand.

The air is sweet with pine and cheer,
With every heartbeat, love draws near.
Crisp laughter mingles with gentle sighs,
Underneath these vast, endless skies.

So let the night be ours to claim,
Beneath the stars, we'll stoke the flame.
In this haven, our spirits soar,
Forever here, we'll seek for more.

Murmurs of the Lone Hunter

In the woods where shadows play,
Echoes of joy at the end of day.
With each step, the whispers speak,
Of bounty found in valley and creek.

The crackle of leaves beneath his feet,
A heart that knows no bitter defeat.
With laughter carried on the breeze,
He finds himself at ease between trees.

Underneath the twilight's veil,
The stars emerge, begin to sail.
With every breath, he feels alive,
In the wild where dreams survive.

As the night unfolds its art,
The hunter knows where to start.
In the murmur of the forest's heart,
He celebrates the night's sweet part.

The Quiet Guardian of the Night

In the quiet of night, a guardian waits,
Holding the magic that softly elates.
With starlight shimmering in his eyes,
He watches over the soft, whispering skies.

Beneath the moon's gentle glow,
He guides lost souls, helping them know.
The beauty in silence, the peace in rest,
In this tranquil realm, hearts are blessed.

The nightingale sings a lullaby sweet,
While crickets play an enchanting beat.
Together they weave a tapestry fine,
As the world rests beneath the pines.

So trust in the quiet, embrace its grace,
Find solace in this tranquil place.
For the guardian's watch will never wane,
In the heart of the night, joy will remain.

Shadows Before Dawn

Shadows whisper as the night retreats,
Colors of dawn bring warmth and beats.
With a hint of gold in the sky's embrace,
Hope awakens, a soft, gentle trace.

The world stirs with the promise of light,
As birds begin their chorus in flight.
In every rustle, a tale unfolds,
Of dreams entwining in marigold.

Together we stand, hand in hand,
United by a love so grand.
With laughter bright and hearts so free,
We're woven into this tapestry.

So let us greet the breaking day,
With joy in our hearts, come what may.
In shadows cast by the morning sun,
A new adventure has just begun.

A Journey into the Unspoken

Whispers of laughter fill the air,
Dancing lights twinkle, unaware.
Colors swirl like dreams untold,
Hearts ignite with joy so bold.

Faces glow in the golden hue,
Echoing memories, old and new.
Every step, a story flows,
In the rhythm where friendship grows.

The night blooms like a fragrant flower,
Each moment counts, we feel the power.
A journey shared, through thick and thin,
Together, let the revelry begin.

Underneath the stars, we gleam,
Lost in a blissful, endless dream.
Our voices rise, a joyous song,
In this festivity, we all belong.

Embrace of the Night Shroud

Glistening shadows cradle the light,
Whispers of secrets leap into sight.
Moonbeams dance on shimmering streams,
As laughter flows through our wildest dreams.

An embrace of night wraps us tight,
Colors blend in the soft twilight.
Stars twinkle in a gentle throng,
In their glow, we sway and belong.

The cool breeze carries a sweet tune,
Guiding hearts beneath the pale moon.
Freedom hums through the open air,
With courage found in love's warm glare.

Every moment a joy to unfold,
In this canvas where life is bold.
Together we weave a tapestry bright,
In the embrace of the magical night.

Songs of the Timid Wanderer

Among the stars, a timid tune,
Echoes softly beneath the moon.
Each note carries a wish untold,
In gentle rhythms, our spirits mold.

With footsteps light on the path we roam,
Finding solace, we create a home.
Laughter bubbles, like a sweet cascade,
In moments shared, our fears all fade.

Our hearts hum in the night's embrace,
Unveiling dreams at a steady pace.
In the glow of each cherished sight,
We sing our songs, hearts shining bright.

Together, we make the shadows flee,
As we wander this jubilee.
In unity, our voices rise,
Like constellations in the skies.

The Langour of Nightfall

As day surrenders to twilight's grace,
Time slows down in this tender place.
With whispers soft, the darkness sighs,
While joy dances beneath the skies.

Candles flicker with a vibrant glow,
Their warmth spreads as the cool winds blow.
In this langour, we find delight,
Wrapped in the love of the starry night.

Feasts adorned with laughter and cheer,
Bringing spirits, both far and near.
In every bite, a taste of glee,
As we savor what it means to be free.

The nightfall gathers; together we stand,
With gratitude woven in every hand.
In the hearts of friends, a flame ignites,
Celebrating life through magical nights.

Veil of the Night's Protector

Underneath the dancing moon,
A canopy of dreams takes flight.
Laughter weaves through velvet blooms,
As shadows greet the joy of night.

Candles flicker, whispers swell,
Stories told by fires bright.
Hearts entwined, all is well,
In the embrace of warm starlight.

Embers glow, the music sways,
Colors swirl in painted air.
Time slips soft in merry ways,
Each moment shared, a treasure rare.

Underneath the night's soft grace,
We find our place; we find our song.
In this realm of sweet embrace,
Together here, we all belong.

Starlight and Solitude

Beneath the vast, eternal dome,
Stars twinkle in their ancient dance.
A tapestry of light, our home,
Fills lonely hearts with a glance.

In the silence, echoes play,
A symphony of dreams takes flight.
Softly, warmth dispels the gray,
As starlight banishes the night.

Wrapped in thoughts like gentle sheets,
We wander through the cosmic sea.
Finding joy in quiet beats,
Reveling in sweet reverie.

When solitude fades, we unite,
Beneath the joy of endless skies.
In starlit glances, we ignite,
A bond that yearns and never dies.

In the Company of Secrets

Whispers float on breezy nights,
Hidden tales of hearts entwined.
In the shadows, dreams take flight,
As passions dance, and souls align.

Through the veils of laughter shared,
Secrets bloom like flowers bright.
In this garden, joys are spared,
Each promise warmed by candlelight.

The world outside fades away,
Here, we revel in our trust.
With playful smiles, we softly play,
Creating magic from the dust.

In this circle, friendships grow,
Through whispered words and knowing glances.
With every heart's delightful glow,
We celebrate life's hidden chances.

The Watcher's Lament

From ancient heights, I see below,
The festival of life unfurls.
A tapestry of joy in flow,
As laughter twirls and music swirls.

Yet in the midst of all this cheer,
A shadow whispers in my soul.
For every smile, a silent tear,
Fleeting moments, beyond control.

I watch the dancers spin their tales,
Their hearts aglow, their spirits bright.
And in my chest, an echo wails,
Longing for warmth, a shared delight.

Still, I raise my glass to the skies,
To fleeting joy and love proclaimed.
For in this world of fleeting sighs,
I stand a watcher, still unclaimed.

Twilight's Watchful Eye

As twilight drapes the sky in gold,
The laughter of friends, a story told.
With lanterns aglow, the shadows dance,
In this moment of magic, we all take a chance.

The whispering breeze carries sweet delight,
While fireflies twinkle in the soft night light.
We gather together, hearts full of cheer,
Celebrating the moments we hold dear.

The stars peek out, one by one,
Under the watch of the setting sun.
In this festive air, we sing and we play,
Embracing the love that won't fade away.

A tapestry woven, with smiles and with grace,
In twilight's embrace, we have found our place.
With joy as our guide, we revel and shine,
In the warmth of each heart, forever entwined.

Between the Pines and Stars

Beneath the pines where shadows lie,
We gather as stars begin to cry.
With laughter and stories shared around,
In this festive haven, joy abounds.

The moon spills silver on the forest floor,
As whispers of magic drift evermore.
With every flicker from the campfire's glow,
Memories blossom, like wildflowers grow.

Voices rise high in a harmonious cheer,
Echoes of laughter, drawing us near.
In the dance of the night, our spirits soar,
Between the pines, we are anything but poor.

Under the vastness of the starlit sea,
We find our hearts beat in unity.
In the tapestry of life, each thread is a rhyme,
Together we shine, for this moment is prime.

Solitary Whispers of the Wilderness

In the stillness of night, whispers roam,
Amongst the trees, nature finds a home.
With the crackle of leaves beneath our feet,
The wilderness beckons, wild and sweet.

Festive echoes of life fill the air,
Songs of the creatures, everywhere.
Under starlit skies, with hearts open wide,
We dance with the shadows, the world our guide.

The cool breeze carries a melody rare,
In this solitude, we find solace there.
With each flicker of stars, our worries we part,
In the wilderness' embrace, we open our heart.

United as one, with the night as our friend,
In the whispers of darkness, we find our blend.
Together we thrive, in this joyous spree,
With nature's symphony, forever free.

Night's Embrace

As night unfurls her velvet shawl,
We gather closely, answering the call.
With lanterns alight and spirits so high,
In this festive embrace, we reach for the sky.

The laughter of children dances on air,
While stories of old bring us all to care.
Each moment a treasure, each smile a flame,
In this night's embrace, we'll never be the same.

The stars share their secrets, twinkling bright,
In this wondrous canvas, pure delight.
With music that flows like a river so wide,
We celebrate life with arms open wide.

In the echo of joy, we find our place,
Wrapped in the magic of night's warm embrace.
With friends all around, our hearts full of glee,
In this festive moment, together we'll be.

Songs of the Hidden Path

In the whispers of the trees, the tunes unfold,
Carried by the breeze, their stories told.
Laughter dances in the light, pure and bright,
As every shadow glimmers, soft and light.

Underneath the arching boughs, we sway,
Colors burst like fireworks, night turns to day.
With each step, the rhythm calls, so sweet,
Together we wander, where the wild heart beats.

In harmony we sing, the echoes call,
With every note, we rise, we never fall.
The hidden path reveals delight anew,
As festive joy blooms in every view.

So let us toast to secrets that we find,
In the heart of nature, where dreams unwind.
With friends and song, we forge our gentle fate,
On this hidden path, we celebrate!

Mysteries of the Darkened Glen

Beneath the canopy, shadows weave,
A tale of joy for all who believe.
Through the twilight, lanterns glow,
In the darkened glen, a vibrant show.

The laughter echoes, a melodic flow,
As spirits dance where the wildflowers grow.
A secret world opens, rich and grand,
Where festivity spins, like grains of sand.

Twinkling stars blink playfully above,
Embracing the night with a mantle of love.
Together we wander, hearts open wide,
In the darkened glen, where dreams coincide.

We lift our cups high, to old tales anew,
In the glow of the fire, as embers accrue.
Where mysteries thrive in the soft, moonlit air,
In this darkened glen, we are free, we are fair.

Encounters with the Soft Howl

Whispers of the night, a soft howl plays,
Guiding us gently through the moonlit maze.
With every step, the world feels alive,
As festive spirits dance, thrive, and strive.

In the glow of the lanterns, shadows prance,
Casting spells of wonder in the night's dance.
The laughter of friends, a melodic chime,
In this sacred moment, we lose track of time.

Each breeze carries stories, shared and dear,
Of warmth and connection, with those we revere.
The soft howl beckons, inviting our cheer,
In the heart of the night, there's nothing to fear.

So let's raise our voices, let joy take flight,
Underneath the stars, our future feels bright.
With each encounter, we weave our sweet tale,
In the symphony of sounds, we shall prevail!

Beneath the Veil of Night

Under the blanket of twinkling stars,
We gather our dreams from near and far.
Laughter spills in whispers, warm and bright,
As we dance together, beneath the night.

The air is filled with magic, soft and clear,
Echoes of joy ring out, drawing us near.
With each step, the rhythm invites us to sway,
In the warmth of the moment, here we'll stay.

Around the fire, stories take flight,
Shared glances ignite the laughter so light.
Each heartbeat resonates with festive zeal,
Beneath the veil of night, we all feel real.

So come and join, let your spirit be free,
In this enclave of joy, just you and me.
As the stars watch over, our hearts ignite,
Together we thrive, beneath the night.

Tides of Silent Reverie

Waves gently whisper, secrets so sweet,
Lost in the moment, where hearts can meet.
Colors of twilight, dance on the shore,
Echoes of laughter, who could ask for more?

Stars peek through clouds, a luminous glow,
Sand between toes, a comforting flow.
The breeze carries joy, with every caress,
Nature's embrace, a soothing success.

Fireflies twinkle, in twilight's embrace,
Stories of wonder, time cannot erase.
Friends all together, sharing delight,
Moments like these, sparkle so bright.

Awash in the magic, the night unfolds,
In tides of reverie, love's warmth enfolds.
Hearts aligned gently, under the sky,
Together we bask, as the night drifts by.

Lullaby of the Hidden Hunter

In the shadowy woods, where secrets abide,
A hunter awaits, with wisdom as guide.
Moonlight dances softly, on leaves overhead,
Nature's sweet lullaby, where dreams are bred.

Whispers of creatures, in nocturnal play,
The heart of the forest will lead them astray.
Under the stars, so brightly they gleam,
A tapestry woven, of life and of dream.

Silence envelops, like a warm, tender shawl,
In shadows we wander, hearing the call.
The night holds its breath, a promise to keep,
Awakening spirits, from tranquil sleep.

The thrill of the chase, in rhythm we find,
Embracing the night, with hearts intertwined.
The lullaby lingers, as dawn starts to break,
In the hush of the woods, our memories awake.

Enchantment of the Moonlit Glade

In a glade bathed in silver, where shadows entwine,
Magic awakens, as stars brightly shine.
Whispers of night air, so soft and divine,
Dancing with fireflies, as hearts intertwine.

The trees sway in rhythm, in joyous delight,
Underneath the vast arch, of glittering light.
Moonbeams spill laughter, casting spells on the ground,
Enchantments aplenty, in the stillness abound.

Beckoning softly, the night calls us near,
Moments of wonder, we hold ever dear.
Together we wander, lost in the glow,
In the enchantment of night, where dreams freely flow.

With each twinkling star, a promise we make,
To cherish the magic, in each little wake.
In the moonlit glade, where time stands so still,
We dance with the shadows, and whisper our will.

To Walk Amongst the Stars

On a pathway of dreams, where stardust is spun,
We tread on the whispers, of worlds yet to come.
Each twinkle above, a tale to unveil,
In the vastness of night, where hopes set sail.

With laughter we journey, on heavenly trails,
Embracing the night air, as our spirit exhales.
The universe beckons, with wonders to share,
An invitation to dance, in the crystal air.

In this cosmic delight, our hearts take flight,
We wander through galaxies, lost in the light.
To walk among stars, is to dream with our eyes,
Where the magic of worlds, eternally lies.

Together we stand, on this luminous shore,
Exploring the beauty, forever in store.
In the night's tender embrace, side by side,
To walk among the stars, let our spirits glide.

Reflections in the Moon's Gaze

In the soft glow, laughter takes flight,
Dancing with stars in the canvas of night.
Whispers of joy in the cool, crisp air,
Moonbeams weaving memories, everywhere.

Candles flicker, casting shadows so bright,
Children's voices, a symphony of delight.
With hearts full of wonder, the night is alive,
In the magic of moments, we truly thrive.

Balloons float gently, under heaven's embrace,
Each smile a tribute to this wondrous space.
Hands held together, we twirl in a dance,
Wrapped in the warmth of this sweet, festive chance.

As the moon smiles down on this gathering place,
Time stands still, lost in joy's sweet grace.
For in this reflection, we find our true song,
In the moon's gentle gaze, we all belong.

The Elusive Stalker

In the twilight whispers, shadows creep,
A quiet thrill that stirs from sleep.
Serenade of night plays soft in the breeze,
Wonders awaken, lost worries cease.

Crickets chant secrets in hushed tones,
While the stars above cast their shimmering moans.
Under the veil of dark's gentle sway,
Laughter erupts in a jubilant display.

The elusive stalker, in masks made of cheer,
Roams through the rooms where all gather near.
Faces aglow with delight and surprise,
In the heart of the night, pure magic lies.

With each cunning glance and teasing jest,
Fires of friendship ignite, manifest.
In this playful chase, let our spirits run free,
For tonight we are bound, in joyous decree.

Shadows of Unbroken Silence

Beneath the stars, in whispers profound,
The shadows awaken without a sound.
Each quiet heartbeat, a tale to unfold,
In the stillness of night, mysteries told.

Glowing lanterns sway, they flicker and beam,
Fragrant flowers dance, lost in a dream.
The cool night wraps us in tender embrace,
As we journey together, each secret to trace.

Gathered around, with hearts intertwined,
In laughter and stories, true bonds we find.
When the night deepens, we shelter the light,
In shadows of silence, we soar, taking flight.

With unbroken moments, we cherish the now,
As the magic enchants, in silence we vow.
To remember this night, this bond we create,
In shadows of silence, we celebrate fate.

The Lore of the Still Night

In the canvas of dusk, tales intertwine,
The lore of the still night, a tale divine.
Moonlit pathways, where stories unfold,
Embracing the night, let the magic enfold.

Stars whisper secrets, so vast and so bright,
Illuminating dreams, a wondrous sight.
Gathered together, we share every cheer,
In the depths of the night, our hearts draw near.

Echoing laughter weaves into the air,
Where joy is the treasure that everyone shares.
In each fleeting glance, and every sweet laugh,
The lore of the still night holds our photograph.

Holding these moments, we raise our refrains,
In the embrace of the night, love reigns.
For the magic of tonight shall always ignite,
The stories we tell in the stillness of night.

The Solace of Nightfall

Stars glow gently in the sky,
Laughter dances, whispers fly.
Joyful hearts in evening's grace,
Together we find our place.

Candles flicker, shadows play,
Dreams unfold, night steals the day.
Underneath the moon's soft light,
We celebrate this tranquil night.

Joyful songs fill the air,
Moments shared, a bond so rare.
In the glow, we are alive,
In our joy, the spirits thrive.

As night deepens, we rejoice,
In the silence, we find our voice.
With smiles bright and hearts so free,
This is where we long to be.

In Search of the Unvoiced

Among the shadows, secrets dwell,
Whispers in the night compel.
Silent wishes floating high,
Dreams that spark like fireflies.

Every glance, a story traded,
In the hush, where love is braided.
Silent moments, softly spun,
In this dance, we are all one.

In the silence, laughter gleams,
Unvoiced thoughts weave vibrant dreams.
Festive hearts, they come alive,
In this space, we laugh and thrive.

Together we seek the unseen,
In the quiet, life is keen.
Voices blend, in joy we roll,
In our souls, we feel it whole.

Hidden Realms of Solitude

Beneath the stars, we roam the night,
In solitude, we find the light.
Moments shared with hearts so true,
In this quiet, joy ensues.

Echoes of laughter, sweet and clear,
In the stillness, we hold dear.
Magical realms, softly revealed,
In our hearts, the truth is sealed.

Time slows down, the world fades away,
In this peace, we long to stay.
Fragrant dreams on gentle breeze,
In our hearts, we find our ease.

As night deepens, we embrace,
In solitude, we find our grace.
Underneath the cosmic glow,
Festive spirits start to flow.

On the Edge of Quietude

At the edge, where silence sings,
Joyful echoes of pure flings.
In the calm, a spark ignites,
We gather close on starry nights.

Fragrant blooms, the air is sweet,
In this moment, hearts will meet.
Colors flash in laughter's glow,
Magic swirls in breezy flow.

Here at dusk, we shed our cares,
Sharing tales of hopes and prayers.
In the quiet, joy abounds,
Whispers weave through merry sounds.

As the night unfolds its charm,
In festive glee, we hold on warm.
Together lost, yet found anew,
In this space, our dreams come true.

Guardian of the Unseen Trail

In the hush of the twilight glow,
A guardian watches, soft and slow.
With twinkling lights that dance and play,
Guiding the lost along their way.

Beneath the stars, a path unwinds,
Echoes of laughter, joy entwined.
Nature's whispers, secrets shared,
With every heartbeat, souls are bared.

Through winter's chill and spring's embrace,
Adventure calls, a thrilling chase.
Paths that weave through trees so tall,
In harmony, we heed the call.

So follow the trail with hearts so light,
The guardian leads us into the night.
With festive cheer and spirits bright,
Together we dance in pure delight.

Solitude in Fur and Fury

In the wild where whispers roam,
A creature of strength calls it home.
With fur like shadows, fierce and proud,
In solitude, it stands unbowed.

The moonlight glimmers on soft eyes,
A guardian spirit in disguise.
Amidst the chaos, calm it brings,
Wrapped in magic of ancient things.

With every rustle, stories weave,
Of dusk's sweet breath, and nights to believe.
Fury and grace entwined in dance,
A festive spirit, a wild romance.

So raise a cheer for all unseen,
For nature's beauty, fierce and keen.
In every heartbeat, joy must flow,
Through fur and fury, life's grand show.

Night's Lurking Mystic

In the shadows where secrets lie,
A mystic lingers, looking sly.
With whispers soft, it calls the night,
Weaving dreams in silver light.

The stars above begin to wane,
In this realm, there's no more pain.
Echoes of laughter dance on air,
Enchanting all who seek, who dare.

As fireflies flicker, a festive tune,
Night's mystic sings beneath the moon.
With every heartbeat, magic swirls,
A tapestry of life unfurls.

So gather 'round, let worries cease,
In this embrace, find joy and peace.
With every shadow, find delight,
In the lurking magic of the night.

Veiled Stalker of the Pines

In twilight's hush, a shadow glides,
A veiled stalker, where mystery hides.
Among the pines, it moves with grace,
A creature born of nature's embrace.

With every step, the forest sighs,
As laughter mingles with soft cries.
Gathered friends in festive cheer,
The spirit of nature, ever near.

Through dappled light and fragrant air,
The stalker weaves with utmost care.
Beneath the stars, it calls us forth,
To celebrate the night's true worth.

So let us roam where wonders thrive,
In the pine-scented dreams, we come alive.
With hearts unbound, we dance and sing,
To the veiled stalker and the joy it brings.

The Shy Spirit of the Northern Wilds

In the hush of the forest's breath,
Dancing lights weave through the trees.
Joyful whispers, a playful jest,
Awakened hearts flutter with ease.

Snowflakes twirl in a silver dance,
Under the gleam of the sparkling stars.
Creatures gather, lost in a trance,
Making wishes on behalf of ours.

A shy spirit peeks from behind,
With a laugh like a gentle breeze.
Sharing secrets, rare and kind,
In this place where the wild hearts tease.

So gather round, as stories unfold,
In the warmth of a bright, crackling fire.
We'll sing of adventures, brave and bold,
And let the night spark our heart's desire.

Whispers of the Moonlit Howl

Beneath the moon's soft, silver glow,
The night comes alive in a sweet embrace.
Winds carry tunes that ebb and flow,
Enchanting rhythms, a magical place.

Wolves gather in a haunting choir,
Their howls weave tales of joy and mirth.
Under the stars, we spark a fire,
Igniting laughter, celebrating worth.

A dance begins on the moistened ground,
Barefoot revelers, hearts entwined.
With every leap, new bonds are found,
In the jubilant echoes, souls combined.

So join us in this moonlit affair,
Where shadows play and spirits rise.
Together we'll wander, float in the air,
Forever caught in the night's surprise.

Echoes of Midnight Prowl

As night drapes softly, the world takes a breath,
Echoes of laughter ripple through the dark.
With whispers and shadows, life teems with zest,
Adventure ignites, igniting a spark.

Footsteps of starlight grace the ground,
Playful spirits flit, weaving through trees.
In this hidden realm, joy knows no bounds,
Where moonbeams dance and hearts find their ease.

A riddle of laughter entwines with the night,
Every corner, a chance to explore.
With friends by our side, everything feels right,
As we indulge in the fun we adore.

So let the midnight prowl be unmissed,
With glee and cheer, the world is our own.
In echoes of joy, memories kissed,
We'll treasure this night, forever our throne.

Secrets in the Shadows

In the cool embrace of twilight's veil,
Secrets dance beneath the trees.
The air is thick with stories to tell,
Carried forth on a lively breeze.

Laughter lingers, a sweet refrain,
Echoing through the quiet night.
As stars chuckle in gentle gain,
We weave our dreams, hearts alight.

With every flicker of candle's glow,
Kindred spirits, side by side.
Embracing joy, we let love flow,
In these shadows, we take our stride.

So gather, friends, in the dim-lit space,
Where secrets flourish beneath the moon.
With every smile, we'll leave a trace,
In the fabric of night, our own sweet tune.

Dusk's Emissary of Quietude

As daylight fades, the world aglow,
Soft whispers dance, where breezes blow.
Lanterns flicker in twilight's embrace,
Joyful hearts find a peaceful space.

Children laugh, as shadows play,
Gathered together, they dream away.
The scent of feasts fills the air,
Laughter echoes, without a care.

Stars begin their gentle twinkle,
Each moment cherished, hearts do crinkle.
With hands held tight, they share the night,
In dusky hues, everything feels right.

A tapestry woven of mirth and cheer,
In this warm haven, all draw near.
Dusk's emissary, so calm and bright,
Bids us to cherish the joyful night.

The Hushed Howl of the Night

The moonlight drapes over fields so wide,
Where nature stirs, and wishes bide.
In hidden corners, secrets rise,
A melodic hum beneath the skies.

Bonfires crackle, stories unfold,
Of feats and dreams, both brave and bold.
Each shared laughter, a sparkling light,
That chases away the chill of night.

Fireflies waltz in an amber glow,
As memories blossom in ebb and flow.
Voices blend in a hushed refrain,
Celebrating joy, easing all pain.

The night wraps around like a soft embrace,
Encouraging wanderlust, a daring chase.
With magic woven into the air,
The hush of twilight, a moment rare.

Lonesome Echoes of Wilderness

Amidst the tall pines, a melody hums,
Echoing softly as twilight comes.
Nature's whispers, wild and free,
Sing songs of life, for you and me.

A moonlit path where shadows sway,
Adventure awaits at the end of the day.
The rustle of leaves, a murmur of peace,
In vast wilderness, our worries cease.

Stars spill light in a crescent arc,
Illuminating paths, igniting sparks.
Around the fire, stories unfold,
Timeless tales of courage retold.

Embrace the magic of wild terrain,
In lonesome echoes, freedom we gain.
Let laughter rise with the whispering breeze,
In nature's heart, our spirits seize.

The Watcher Beneath Starry Skies

Under a blanket of deep midnight blue,
The stars twinkle bright, a radiant view.
Each light a wish, a dream set free,
Connected in silence, you and me.

The night unfolds with twinkling glee,
As constellations dance and sing of spree.
A symphony of stars paints the night,
In their gentle glow, we find delight.

With thoughts like comets, racing across,
In the vast expanse, there's never loss.
The watcher smiles, lost in the glow,
Finding solace where wild wonders flow.

Gathered together, hearts open wide,
In the cosmos', we freely glide.
Beneath starry skies, life's dreams align,
In this festive moment, your hand in mine.

A Dance of Silent Footsteps

In twilight's glow, the whispers rise,
With lantern beams like twinkling skies.
The shadows waltz, they weave and twine,
Beneath the stars, where hearts align.

The laughter rings, a gentle tune,
As fireflies dance beneath the moon.
A gathering lost from day's embrace,
In every smile, a warm grace.

Footsteps soft on the mossy ground,
In the night's balm, friendship found.
With every twirl, in dreams we soar,
Together weaving tales of yore.

And as the dawn begins to break,
In silent joy, our hearts awake.
A dance we'll share, forever spun,
In the light of another sun.

Secrets of the Ivy-Crowned Earth

Beneath the boughs, where shadows play,
The ivy whispers of the day.
A hidden realm, alive and bright,
Where secrets bloom in morning light.

The petals blush with colors bold,
As stories of the earth unfold.
In every rustle, every sigh,
The laughter of the trees floats high.

With friends beside, we delve so deep,
Into the roots where old ones sleep.
A tapestry of life so grand,
Beneath the earth, we take our stand.

And in this fest, where nature sings,
We find the joy that friendship brings.
In ivy's crown, our hearts entwined,
A bond of secrets, sweetly signed.

The Hidden Call of the Wild

In the rustling leaves, a song begins,
A call to dance where freedom spins.
The wild invites with open arms,
A tapestry of nature's charms.

With every sunrise, the earth awakes,
Beneath the canopy, the heartbeat breaks.
The animals join in a merry tune,
Under the watchful gaze of the moon.

Companions gather, our spirits soar,
With every step, we want for more.
Through fields of green, the laughter flows,
In this wild world, our love just grows.

Every whisper speaks of adventure vast,
In the chorus of the present and past.
Together we roam, through woods and glades,
In the wild's embrace, our joy cascades.

Solitude in the Deep Forest

In the forest's heart, a quiet place,
Among the trees, time finds its grace.
The breeze holds secrets, soft and sweet,
Where silence blooms and wonders meet.

With gentle steps on the forest floor,
The echoes of nature, a soothing score.
The sunlight spills like golden wine,
In solitude, our souls align.

Here in the stillness, a joy we seek,
The whispers of the leaves, so unique.
With every breath, a story told,
In this deep forest, memories unfold.

And as the twilight drapes its veil,
In harmony, our hearts set sail.
For in this peace, we truly find,
The festive light that threads our mind.

The Solitary Serenade

Under a starlit sky, the nightbirds sing,
Melodies of joy, in soft winds they bring.
A gentle breeze carries whispers so sweet,
Dancing like embers, where hearts gently meet.

Laughter of crickets fills the air with cheer,
Celebrating life, as the moon draws near.
Each note a promise, each chord a delight,
In the solitude, the world feels just right.

With fireflies twinkling, like stars they ignite,
A tapestry woven from shadows and light.
Life's simple pleasures, in harmony blend,
A serenade played, where echoes transcend.

In this moonlit wonder, worries take flight,
The solitary serenade blooms in the night.
Here in the stillness, the heart finds its tune,
With joy everlasting, beneath the bright moon.

Eyes of the Timid Night Watcher

In the hush of twilight, where shadows reside,
A timid soul watches as day starts to hide.
With eyes wide and bright, absorbing the glow,
Of lanterns and stardust, in soft, tender flow.

The pulse of the night wraps its arms around,
Each whispering breeze, a comforting sound.
As laughter of children dances down the lane,
With hope in their voices, dispelling all pain.

The moon watches over, a guardian true,
Casting dreamlike spells with its silvery hue.
The heart of the night beats with rhythm and grace,
In shadows, the timid now finds their warm place.

Embracing the magic, they settle in close,
With every soft sparkle, their spirit will boast.
Eyes of the timid, now gleaming with light,
Together they flourish in the care of the night.

The Unheard Chorus of Nature

In the forest's embrace, where whispers entwine,
The unheard chorus fills the air, divine.
Leaves sway and shimmer, in sync with the breeze,
Nature's sweet symphony echoes with ease.

River's gentle flow sings a lullaby sweet,
While crickets compose in their rhythmic retreat.
An orchestra hidden, but vibrant and clear,
Brimming with life, it draws all ever near.

With every soft rustle, the world comes alive,
A dance of the creatures, where magic will thrive.
Flowers bloom boldly, their colors a spark,
Unseen, yet felt deeply, from daylight to dark.

As night softly blankets the vibrant display,
The unheard chorus hums night into day.
In nature's own rhythm, hearts learn to confide,
In the heart of the wild, where dreams coincide.

Secrets Wrapped in Silver Fur

Among the frosty pines, a secret does dwell,
Wrapped in silver fur, with a shimmering spell.
Creatures in shadows, with eyes bright and bold,
Guard the whispered tales that the wilds have told.

With footsteps like whispers, they glide through the night,

Chasing the moonbeams, pure and white.
In the still of the dark, wonders silently stir,
As stars twinkle softly, with secrets to confer.

Each flick of a tail, a language profound,
Echoes of laughter in the silence resound.
The frost-kissed leaves sing of magic unseen,
In a world only ventured by the brave and the keen.

Together they gather, those souls wrapped in dreams,
Unveiling the stories that sparkle and gleam.
Secrets wrapped tenderly in nature's embrace,
Forever enchanting, in this serene space.

A Shroud of Midnight Fog

In twilight's cloak, the lights ignite,
The laughter echoes through the night.
With whispered tales from distant shores,
A magic dance that never bores.

Around the fire, faces gleam,
In shadows, we weave our shared dream.
Chasing the glow of fleeting moments,
Unraveling joy, like bright components.

As fog embraces every smile,
We wander freely, mile by mile.
In the stillness, hearts combine,
In midnight's fog, we intertwine.

With every cheer, our spirits rise,
Under the vast, enchanting skies.
In every glance, a spark ignites,
In this shroud, the world feels bright.

The Dreamer Beneath the Stars

Beneath the velvet canopy's gleam,
We find the space where wishes dream.
Glowing orbs in endless flight,
Guide us through this festive night.

With every laugh, we share a tale,
Spinning yarns like silver sail.
In whispers soft, the secrets flow,
As starlit glances start to glow.

Around us, scents of sweetest cheer,
The warmth of friendship drawing near.
Hands joined in a delicate waltz,
In tune with magic, filled with pulse.

And under the stars, we raise a glass,
To fleeting moments, may they last.
In this realm, where dreams align,
With every heartbeat, joy we find.

Lament of the Mysterious Realm

In shadows deep, the echoes sigh,
Of wishes cast in nights gone by.
With lanterns bright, we chase the light,
Through veils of time that blend the night.

A tapestry of dreams unfolds,
With whispered secrets yet untold.
The hills alive with distant song,
In this strange place, where we belong.

The night unveils its mystic art,
As every star plays its sweet part.
In the distance, laughter rings,
A symphony of gentle things.

We dance beneath the watchful eyes,
Of moonlit clouds in azure skies.
In every twirl, we lose the fear,
In this mystery, joy draws near.

Guardian of Unspoken Stories

Amidst the crowd, a figure stands,
With silent tales in gentle hands.
Each glance a window to the past,
Each heartbeat echoes, deep and vast.

With every nod, a spark ignites,
And laughter floats on breezy nights.
In subtle shadows, truths reside,
As whispers guide the heart inside.

In the fireplace, stories glow,
Like embers dancing to and fro.
In every pause, a world anew,
The guardian speaks with tales for few.

With every beat of night's soft heart,
We craft the tales, we play our part.
In unity, we shape and mold,
Unspoken stories, rich and bold.

Solitary Footprints in the Snow

In a blanket white, a path unfolds,
Each footprint a story, a memory holds.
Joy dances in flakes, swirling around,
A whispering laughter, in silence resound.

The world is a canvas, so bright and so pure,
Creating a cheer, a spirit demure.
With every step forward, the heart beats bold,
In festive delight, as the winter unfolds.

Snowmen and angels, both joyous and free,
Children engaging in playful decree.
A snowball uproar, laughter in the air,
Frosty enchantment, a jubilant flair.

The moonlight sparkles, igniting the night,
In solitary footprints, life feels so right.
With every soft crunch, the magic ignites,
In the snowy embrace, our spirits take flight.

A Heartbeat in the Stillness

In the hush of the night, where shadows reside,
A heartbeat resounds, like the ocean's tide.
Stars gleam like jewels, in the deep velvet blue,
Whispers of wonder, a symphony true.

With every soft breath, the world feels alive,
A festive sensation, where dreams can derive.
Laughter and joy weave through the calm air,
In the magic of stillness, there's love everywhere.

The flicker of lights, like fireflies dance,
In the heart of the night, we sway and we prance.
A gathering of warmth, where all spirits meet,
Creating a story, pure and sweet.

Together we linger, bound by the glow,
A heartbeat in stillness, a beautiful flow.
In this tender moment, let happiness spill,
For in the silence, our hearts feel the thrill.

Moonlit Secrets of the Silent Hunter

Beneath the full moon, a shadow glides through,
The silent hunter, with purpose anew.
Whispers of night, secrets held tight,
As stars overhead begin their descent, oh what a sight!

In the stillness and calm, adventure ignites,
With a heart filled with courage, as magic invites.
The forest alive, with creatures of night,
In the mystery and wonder, our spirits take flight.

The rustle of leaves is a sweet serenade,
In the abyss of darkness, we're unafraid.
Each heartbeat a rhythm, a dance with the night,
Celebrating existence, in the soft silver light.

Together we cherish the secrets we find,
In the moonlit beauty, our hearts intertwined.
With joy in our steps and laughter so near,
Life's festive enchantment, forever sincere.

The Enigma of the Lone Chaser

In the mist of the dawn, a figure appears,
The lone chaser runs, leaving behind fears.
With every swift stride, the world starts to fade,
In pursuit of a dream, unafraid and unmade.

The sun rises golden, illuminating wide,
Chasing shadows and secrets, with joy as his guide.
Forest and skyline, the road twists and turns,
In his heart, a flame of passion that burns.

Laughter of echoes, a beckoning song,
As he dances with clouds, where he feels he belongs.
In the spirit of movement, freshness prevails,
Creating adventure, where joy never fails.

The enigma unfolds, in each boundless chase,
Fostering wonder, in a jubilant race.
With laughter and light, the chase finds its way,
A festive embrace, welcoming the day.

Elegy of the Moonlit Forest

In the glow of the silver night,
Whispers dance among the leaves,
Stars wink from heights of delight,
Nature sings as the heart believes.

Laughter echoes through the trees,
Creatures revel in moon's embrace,
The melody floats on the breeze,
Each shadow wears a joyful face.

Fires crackle, warmth in the air,
Stories shared under the stars,
Glimmers of joy everywhere,
Binding souls with invisible bars.

As the night wraps in its gown,
We twirl in time, lost in the song,
In the forest, no one wears a crown,
In our hearts, we all belong.

Echoes of a Hidden Truth

In corners where secrets are kept,
Laughter breaks through the quiet night,
Among the shadows, silence crept,
Yet whispers bring stories to light.

A gathering of souls, so bright,
With eyes that sparkle like the dawn,
Friendship blooms in the soft twilight,
In every stride, new bonds are drawn.

Beneath the swaying willow tree,
Memories weave a vibrant thread,
In the fabric of unity,
Hopes shared for the paths ahead.

Echoes linger long after they part,
Joyful tales of what's yet to be,
In our hearts, an unbreakable heart,
Together we paint life's tapestry.

Legends of the Starlit Savanna

Beneath a tapestry of dreams,
The savanna breathes with life,
Stars like lanterns cast their beams,
Whispers carry the tales of strife.

In the haze of the night's embrace,
Dance of shadows, wild and free,
Echoes of laughter fill the space,
A celebration of unity.

Colors of dusk blend and swirl,
A canvas painted bold and bright,
Every spirit, every girl,
Find solace in this joyous night.

With every rhythm, hearts beat strong,
Legends of old meet the new,
In the savanna, where we belong,
Our story forever shines through.

The Unseen Tread

Through fields of gold the shadows slip,
A melody hangs in the air,
The earth beneath feels every trip,
Celebrations weave moments rare.

Faint echoes guide the way we trod,
Laughter flowing like a stream,
Joy resides in every nod,
In this trance, we chase our dream.

Bright lanterns sway with gentle grace,
Glinting eyes reflect the glow,
In this festive, enchanted space,
We find the treasures that we sow.

As the night drapes its velvet cloak,
We join in song, hearts unconfined,
Each unseen tread a word spoke,
In this dance, our spirits entwined.

The Stealthy Dance in Shadows

In the glow of the moonlight bright,
Figures twirl, a graceful sight.
Silhouettes leap through the night,
Echoes of joy take flight.

With laughter woven in the air,
Dancers spin without a care.
Whispers tease the evening's cheer,
Magic's touch is truly near.

The stars blink in sweet delight,
As shadows blend with vibrant light.
A symphony of heartbeats plays,
In endless, joyous displays.

Beneath the canopy so wide,
Unity flows like the tide.
Innocence found in each glance,
Together lost in this dance.

Quiet Footfalls on Ancient Trails

Through the woods, where echoes roam,
Footsteps whisper, finding home.
Leaves flutter, a greeting brief,
In the shelter, find relief.

Candles flicker, soft and warm,
Nature's pulse, a soothing balm.
Path of dreams in moonlit grace,
Each step brings a new embrace.

Songs of rivers hum along,
Wrap the night in nature's song.
Stars align with silent goals,
Filling hearts and warming souls.

Here beneath the mighty trees,
Feel the magic in the breeze.
A tapestry of ancient lore,
Whispers beckon, come explore.

The Phantom of the Evergreen

In a grove where spirits play,
Softly shimmers night and day.
Evergreen, a sentinel,
Holds the secrets that they tell.

Moonlit paths where shadows glide,
Amidst the branches, dreamers hide.
Elusive, like a fleeting thought,
Each echo weaves what time forgot.

Dance of leaves, a gentle sigh,
As the phantom flits nearby.
Playful whispers, wild and free,
Every heartbeat's mystery.

In this haven, free from fear,
Joy and laughter fill the sphere.
With every swirl, a tale unfolds,
Of ageless wonder, brightly told.

Whispers of the Woodland Guardian

By the light of dawn's embrace,
Nature's keeper dwells in grace.
Gentle rustles, voices soft,
Guide the wanderers aloft.

Guardian of each vibrant tree,
Speaks in tones of harmony.
Breezes carry tales unknown,
In the woods, we find our home.

With the dawn, the silence breaks,
Every creature gently wakes.
A tapestry of life appears,
Dancing through the passing years.

Vibrant blooms and laughter blend,
Magic stirs, the heart to mend.
Whispers flow, a sacred trust,
In this realm, we live, we must.